Papal Bull

Dean Sullivan

Illustrated by
Pete Bastiansen

818.
54
SUL

TROCAIRE COLLEGE
Buffalo

D1166129

meadowbrook
Distributed by Simon & Schuster
New York, New York

**Library of Congress
Cataloging-in-Publication Data**

Sullivan, Dean
Papal bull / by Dean Sullivan
1. Catholic wit and humor.
I. Title.
PN6231.C22S94 1988 818'.5402—dc19
88-11953
ISBN 0-88166-115-5
Copyright ©1988 by Dean Sullivan

Edited by Joseph Oberle and Bruce Lansky
Illustrated by Pete Bastiansen

All rights reserved. No part of this book may
be reproduced in any form without written
permission from the publisher, except in the
case of brief quotations embodied in critical
articles and reviews.

Published by Meadowbrook, Inc.
18318 Minnetonka Boulevard
Deephaven, MN 55391

BOOK TRADE DISTRIBUTION by Simon &
Schuster, a division of Simon & Schuster Inc.
1230 Avenue of the Americas
New York, NY 10020

S & S Ordering #: 0-671-67085-9

88 89 90 91 92 10 9 8 7 6 5 4 3 2 1

Printed in the United States of America

Dedication

To Mom and Dad, for all you've done, and some of the things you haven't.

Acknowledgments

I would like to thank all the people who helped me creatively and put up with me personally in order to complete *Papal Bull*. These include the contributing writers, none of whom I've met, all of whom I appreciate. Also, Patricia McKernon who started the editorial ball moving.

Keeping that ball rolling was Sheryl Otterson, who held the project together as the production editor and earned my gratitude and respect, whether she wants them or not.

Finally, there are two more people to whom I owe thanks. Bruce Lansky gave me a great opportunity, and Joe Oberle made sure I didn't blow it. If there are some I have forgotten, I'm sorry, and consider yourselves thanked. Thanks.

Introduction

You spent a long Saturday night out on the town or up with the late show. Now you're looking forward to sleeping late and eating a leisurely breakfast. Suddenly, there's a scratch at your door and you remember: It's Sunday. Sticking your head under the pillow won't do you any good. Hiding under the bed is useless. It's the Sabbath and the Mass Hounds have tracked you down.

When you're Catholic a Mass Hound can come in a variety of breeds. It can be a parent ("Get out of bed now or get out of the house later"); a loving spouse ("Wake up dear, or sleep on the couch tonight"); a high-horsed roommate ("I'm going to Mass. Are you just going to lie there all day?"); or a younger sibling ("I've got him cornered in here, Dad!"). The most persistent Mass Hound may be your conscience, which always knows where you are—and where you should be. In one form or another, you can be sure the Mass Hounds will eventually bay at your window.

Catholics accept the Mass Hounds and mandatory Mass attendance because we believe it makes us better than the other religions. And let's face it, it can't hurt! Unfortunately, feeling high and mighty doesn't make it any easier to trade a feathery mattress for a pew as hard as a three-day-old Host. But *Papal Bull* just might.

Papal Bull is not a book that will reaffirm your faith, but it *will* redefine it. Slip it into your pocket or purse before you go to Mass and slip it out after you've read the bulletin for the third time. Think of it as educational. Think of it as a religious experience. Think of it as the priest drones into the twentieth minute of his sermon. Little kids get to bring books to Mass, why should they have all the fun?

The best thing is you don't have to worry about God striking you down for reading *Papal Bull* during Mass. I wrote practically the whole book there and I'm still around. The Mass Hounds make sure of that.

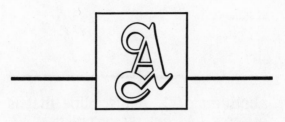

abbey A place where the miniskirt may never catch on.

abbot The man who decides who's on first at the annual monastery softball game.

Abel A son of Adam who was also ready and willing.

abortion Damned if you do, mommed if you don't.

Abraham "Father of many," uncle of a Lot.

absolution Music to your errs.

abstinence 1. A discipline that is oft-preached but rarely practiced. 2. What makes the heart grow fonder, the body grow hungrier, and the spirit grow grouchier. 3. A no-know (in the biblical sense).

accommodation When a theologian interprets scripture to suit his own needs, like when Jimmy Swaggart accused Jim Bakker of consorting with a prostitute.

acolyte A low calorie altar boy.

act of contrition A penitential prayer you warm up with so you don't cramp up in the confessional.

act of faith An action that shows a person's belief that an event will occur—such as when a guy cleans his bedroom before a big date.

act of God 1. The kind of disaster insurance doesn't cover. 2. The only way to get some Catholics to church on Sunday.

Acts of the Apostles 1. Phony motions to the wallet made by the Apostles when the check arrived for the Last Supper. 2. Christ's touring company—they knocked'em dead in Samaria, Thessalonica, Damascus, etc.

Adam The first man to fall for a woman.

adultery An extracurricular activity no one wants to letter in.

Advent A season filled with the sounds of pipers piping, drummers drumming, and cash registers ringing.

Advent wreath A brightly colored, seasonally decorated fire hazard.

---

agnostic   1. An atheist who is hedging his bets. 2. Someone who isn't sure if there is a God, but who *is* sure he doesn't want to go to Mass every Sunday.

Agony in the Garden   Why sandals were invented.

All Saints' Day (November 1st) A day to honor the least-known saints and give your least-liked Halloween candy to your little brother.

All Souls' Day (November 2nd) The day to remember all deceased Motown recording artists.

alms What, along with your legs, the church expects in the collection plate on Sunday.

alpha and omega The fraternity that Christ belonged to.

altar boys/girls Servers kept awake by hot, dripping candle wax.

amen The only part of a prayer everyone knows.

Anabaptists Members of a sect that prohibits baptism until adulthood—whose growth is inhibited because they don't get 'em while they're young.

angels Spiritual beings who hold their sock hops on the head of a pin.

annulment 1. Divorce, Catholic style. 2. A decree that a marriage never existed—like the dream sequence on "Dallas."

Antichrist A pseudo-savior who would give a blind man the address of a good optometrist.

Apocalypse An important event that you probably can't find a Hallmark card for.

Apocrypha The books that were deleted from the New Testament. For example, the First Letter of Paul to Himself: "Take out trash, send tunic to laundry, save Thessalonica." (Him. 1:1-3)

apostasy The difficult process of giving up one set of beliefs in favor of another—such as converting to the metric system.

Apostles Christ's closest disciples, and the twelve names your mother yells at you until she gets yours right.

Apostles' Creed When you consider the betrayal of Judas, the denial of Peter, and the doubting of Thomas, it's not exactly the "Code of the Old West."

apostolic bull What Peter was caught slinging before the rooster crowed three times.

apostolic succession   The schedule that determined when each of the Twelve got to sit next to Jesus at supper.

archangel   An angel who can't fly straight.

Ark of the Covenant   The trajectory of the tablets when Moses threw them down the mountain.

Armageddon   The last day you can redeem your green stamps.

Ascension of Christ Jesus rose into heaven forty days after Easter—an indication of how tough it is to get a table up there.

asceticism Living a pure, virtuous life—and then dying of boredom.

Ash Wednesday The day Catholics spend telling non-Catholics that it's not dirt on their foreheads.

Assumption of Mary Another reason Joseph didn't purchase a family plot.

"As ye sow, so shall ye reap." A phrase depicting the story of the neverending clothing repair that a Catholic mother must face. In other words: "As I sew, so shall they rip."

atheist 1. One who denies the existence of God and probably spends very little time in foxholes. 2. Someone who doesn't say "God bless you" when you sneeze.

atonement What Catholics achieve every Sunday after an ordeal of sitting, kneeling, and standing.

auxiliary bishops Relief preachers.

avarice The cardinal sin you can't get enough of.

Ave Maria Mary's mailing address.

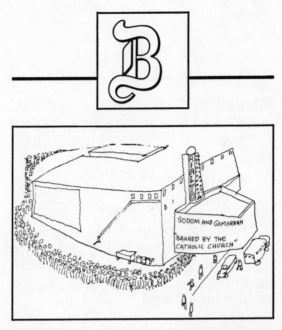

ban How the Church makes box-office smashes out of objectionable movies.

banns of marriage A final plea for help before taking the plunge.

Baptists The kids at municipal swimming pools who are always dunking each other.

Barabbas The criminal who should have been accompanied by a couple of first-round draft choices in the Christ trade.

beatification 1. Papal recognition that a holy person is one step away from having a parochial school named after him. 2. The step in the canonization process when a person's head is fitted for a halo.

beatitudes 1. Sayings that look nice on a cross-stitched plaque. 2. Second-rate attitudes.

Beelzebub Satan's right-horned man.

benediction The start of the race to the parking lot.

Bethlehem Where Mary and Joseph had to come to their census.

Bible The greatest story ever told ... though it would still have ratings trouble against Cosby.

Bible Belt What some TV evangelists are in need of.

biblical times When getting to know someone was a pleasure.

bigamy 1. When it doesn't matter which side of the bed you wake up on in the morning. 2. Proof that two wrongs don't make a right.

bingo 1. How Catholics tithe. 2. The parlor game churches organize each week to keep little old ladies off the street.

bishop   Old man in the see.

black smoke   The signal that either a new Pope has not yet been selected or the cardinals have burned their dinner.

blasphemy   Spreading a rumor that your church buys its Hosts at a day-old shop.

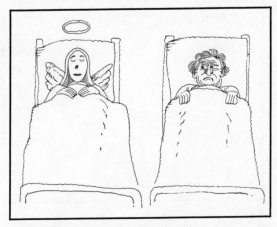

Blessed Virgin The phrase Joseph muttered himself to sleep with.

blessing A prayer preceding an event that grants God's grace and releases Him from any liability.

blind faith A redundant expression.

Body of Christ Amen ... oops, sorry. Habit, I guess.

bulletin 1. Parish information read only during the homily. 2. Catholic air-conditioning. 3. Your receipt for attending Mass.

burning bush What the Israelites thought Moses had been smoking when he said he spoke with God.

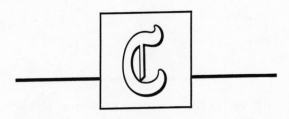

Caiaphas Co-Pilate.

Cain The blunt instrument with which Abel was bludgeoned.

Calvin, John The man who championed the theory of predestination—whether he wanted to or not.

candle What you should light instead of cursing the darkness and kicking the dog.

canonization An honor posthumously bestowed upon a person who lived an exemplary life—although many saints might have preferred receiving a gold watch and a plaque of appreciation at sixty-five.

Canon Law The principle that whoever has the canon makes the law.

---

capital sins More serious than lowercase sins.

cardinal A bishop with connections.

carnal knowledge Knowing there is a hamburger in the house as you bite into a fish stick during Lent.

caroling 1. A Christmas tradition of walking from house to house singing yule songs until residents give you food to shut you up. 2. Yuletide revenge on the neighbor whose barking dog keeps you awake nights.

cassock 1. The dress-like garment worn by altar boys that's black and white and makes them red all over. 2. An altar garment that could cause a server to commit a messy foot fault.

catacombs A maze of grace.

---

catechism A manual that boils down to "God is good, but don't press your luck."

cathedral Where you should watch out for low-flying buttresses.

Catholic Someone who has a better chance at becoming Pope than President.

Catholicism A religion based on the firm belief in the Kingdom of God, the Divinity of Christ, the authority of the Pope, and the family-size bottle of ketchup.

Catholic Mass An event with so much standing, sitting, and kneeling you can forego your Jane Fonda aerobic workout for Sunday.

Catholic wedding A ceremony at which a father loses his daughter—and his life savings.

celebrant   The host with the Host.

celibacy   A clever comeback used by single men and women to explain why they didn't have a date Saturday night.

cemetery   1. Where it's hard for people to keep their composure. 2. Where there's a stiff fine for trespassing.

censer What a priest likes to light up after a good meal.

chalice A wine stein.

chancery The business office of the Church—even God needs help with His taxes.

changing water into wine The reason that the Apostles would clear the shower room when Jesus came in.

charismatics People who heal by faith, speak in tongues, and provide titillating headlines for supermarket tabloids.

charity 1. What you call your trash when you give it to the Little Sisters of the Poor. 2. The only one of the three theological virtues that pays off every April 15th.

chastity The vow that keeps sisters and brothers from becoming mommies and daddies.

children of God What we all are, so nyaah!

choir A group of people whose singing allows the rest of the congregation to lip-sync.

christening The ceremony that gets your head wet in the Church and your feet wet in Catholicism.

Christians People who follow Jesus, although they disagree on which way He went.

Christmas The celebration of the birth of Christ, which invariably falls during the busiest shopping season of the year.

Christmas tree   The dry, brown, prickly thing that usually gets thrown out with the New Year's resolutions.

church   The only place besides elevators where people face forward and say nothing to each other.

Church Expectant (the Church in purgatory)   Being stuck between God and a hot place.

Church Militant (the Church on earth)   A boring mass during which the distractions occur two minutes apart.

Church of Christ, Scientist A sect whose members believe Jesus is good for what ails you.

Church Triumphant (the Church in Heaven) When the parish softball team beats the beanies off the neighborhood synagogue.

circumcision A Jewish religious custom that Catholics practice so their sons won't be embarrassed in locker-room showers.

Cleansing of the Temple When Christ mopped up His Father's house with a bunch of merchants.

cloister A cross between the clergy and an oyster.

---

coat of many colors The hand-me-down sports jacket that you wore for your First Communion.

cohabitation Living together without benefit of clergy or threat of in-laws.

collection Pennies for Heaven.

collection envelope Something you won't get back marked "Return to Sender."

College of Cardinals An institution where you might see pranks like fish stick swallowing and confessional stuffing.

colosseum 1. A Christian's last stop before the mausoleum. 2. The site of the Christian Bowl (or, from the lion's point of view, a bowl of Christians).

---

concelebration Synchronized preaching.

confession What you bragged about the night before.

confessional The sin-rescind bin.

confession, bad When the priest falls asleep while you're recounting your sins.

confession, good When the priest brings in the deacon to listen.

conscience The little voice of morality that you wish had a body so you could punch it in the nose.

contraception A device that is used by people who don't want to kid around.

contraceptive A rubber banned.

convent A rectory where the toilet seats are always down.

conversion The point-after-touchdown scored at a parish football game by the newly baptized kicker.

corona The goofy haircut some monks receive to ensure their vow of chastity.

covenant A contract between God and His people—one that the Devil is still trying to take to arbitration.

creation The story that scientists get a big bang out of.

creationism The belief that no one is a monkey's uncle.

cremation Making an ash of yourself.

crosier The hooked staff a bishop carries—perfect for hauling sinners into the confessional.

crown of thorns A rose by any other name is still a rose—but as a hat, it hurts.

crucifix A cross hung as a reminder that Christ died for our sins, so we should be good, that's about as effective a deterrent as a UN sanction.

crucifixion 1. A rather extreme form of impeachment. 2. The form of Roman execution used when the lions were full.

cry room A place in the back of the church where children are brought after their tantrums have reduced their parents to tears.

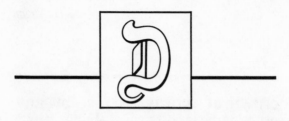

damn A term that means Hell *and* high water.

David A Jewish king who today would be subjected to urinalysis.

Dead Sea Scrolls The Cliffs Notes to the Old Testament.

Delilah The woman who made things a little hairy for Samson.

denial In a poll of sinners, the sin they claimed to commit the least.

despair The sin that is said to be the worst—as if you don't already have enough to feel down about.

Devil Evil with a capital *D*.

devotion Standing for the duration of the Gospel on Palm Sunday.

disciples Followers of Christ who hadn't earned enough merit badges to become Apostles.

divine intervention What happens when God steps in and does something for the good of mankind ... like ending Ronald Reagan's movie career.

divorce The legal dissolution of a marriage that is not recognized by the Church—which believes there is nothing civil about matrimony.

dogma Church doctrine that is revealed by God, pronounced by the Pope, and considered infallible—until one of the two changes His mind.

Dona Nobis Pacem The double-play combination on the parish softball team.

Doubting Thomas A person who, when he reads that Jesus walked on the water, believes He knew where the rocks were.

doxology A verbal high-five with the Lord.

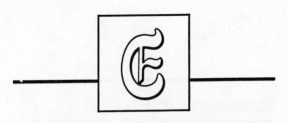

earthly life The minor leagues, from which Catholics hope to get called up.

Easter 1. The day that you see Catholics you haven't seen since Christmas. 2. The day when Christ's body is missing and all the children are worried about is finding the missing chocolate eggs.

Ecumenical Council Where all those "a priest, a rabbi, and a minister" jokes get started.

ecumenical prayer service When Christians of various denominations get together and confuse the heck out of God.

ecumenism The practice of unity among Christians whereby Catholics cut Protestants some slack for being close.

Egypt The country which created the first form of writing: hieroglyphics—the basis for all medical prescriptions.

Ember Days Special days of fasting—for instance, when you're camping and you can't get the fire going.

encyclical Proof that what goes around doesn't necessarily come around.

end of the world When the Cubs win the World Series.

Enlightenment The period right after the Dark Ages when everyone walked around squinting.

envy The sin Catholics commit when they think of non-Catholics who get to remain seated during their church services.

Epiphany The commemoration of the coming of the Magi, celebrated January 6 because of New Year's Eve hangovers.

Episcopalians Upwardly mobile Protestants.

epistle How Christian troubleshooters tried to clean up those heathen, one-camel towns.

eschatology The study of scriptures predicting final events in the history of the world—such as the Second Coming of Christ, married clergy, and female priests.

eternity The time between Communion and the end of Mass.

Eucharist Definitely not a disciple of Bob Uecker.

evangelists, TV 1. Preachers with miraculous power—the ability to squeeze dollars out of the penniless. 2. Men of prey.

Eve The only wife who never had to worry about the "other woman."

everlasting life   1. What a Catholic will need to understand all the changes since Vatican II. 2. A phenomenon best exhibited by Dick Clark.

evil   Four-fifths of the Devil.

excommunicant   Someone who's been banished to watching football games on Sundays.

excommunication   What happens when the parish phone is cut off by the telephone company.

exorcism   Scaring the hell out of someone.

eye for an eye   Rule of thumb when the other guy is smaller.

eye of the needle   The analogy that provides a strong incentive for rich men to breed tiny camels.

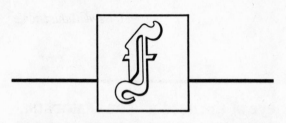

faith Giving God the benefit of the doubt on the question "Can God make a rock so big that even He, Himself, cannot lift it?"

fall of man When Adam slipped on an apple peel.

false god   The idol young Catholics pray to during a true-false test.

false witness   The kind you can find on "People's Court."

fast   God's diet plan.

fear of God   1. Dread of a lightning bolt with your name on it. 2. A more serious concept than that "you better not pout" stuff Bing Crosby croons about.

Feast of the Ascension   The holy day observed forty days after Easter, by which time all the black jelly beans should be gone.

feed the five thousand   What a Catholic mother has to do for Easter dinner.

fire and brimstone The type of sermon that inspires people to fly right—at least until the weekend.

First Communion 1. The day Catholic kids stop reading bible story books during Mass and start reading the bulletin. 2. Another in a long line of religious celebrations that give your parents a reason to throw a party.

First Communion candle What comes in handy during an electrical storm.

First Confession   When you lay the groundwork for the next one.

fishers of men   A description of the Apostles who trawled for souls.

folk mass   The type of liturgy celebrated at the church of Saints Peter, Paul, and Mary.

font   The baptismal basin where the priest wets the baby's head and the baby wets the priest's vestments.

fortitude   The inner strength that keeps you in Mass until the end, even though you're missing the kickoff.

Forty Hours' Devotion   Harder than spending the weekend with the in-laws.

Four Evangelists   The original Fab Four who started the Christian Invasion.

Four Horsemen of the Apocalypse
The crew that you wouldn't hire as the pony ride at your child's birthday party.

frankincense   A biblical condiment for hot dogs.

Freemason Someone who will fix the church steps for nothing.

free will A gift from God that you will pay for later if you use it incorrectly.

Friday, Good The day of the crucifixion of Jesus—which makes you wonder what a Messiah's got to do to make it Bad Friday.

fundamentalist option The type of offense employed by the seminary football team.

Garden of Eden Where Adam and Eve dug us a hole.

Gentiles People put on earth because *someone* has to buy retail.

genuflection The reason the right pant leg of a Catholic is more worn than the left.

gluttony Getting in the Communion line for seconds.

Gnosticism Gneo-Christian cult based on gnebulous gnosis, whose days were gnumbered due to gnaysayers.

god A minor-league deity.

TROCAIRE COLLEGE
Buffalo, New York 14220

God   The Supreme Being who knows everything, including why the Howells brought so many clothes for a three-hour tour.

godparent   A person who has to baby-sit on request.

Godspell   The spelling bee that can get you out of purgatory—if you can spell words like Ecclesiasticus and Melchizedek.

gold   The only gift of the Magi that Mary didn't return.

Golden Rule   The most painful thing a nun can hit you with.

Good Samaritan   A guy who today would probably get arrested and left in jail until "60 Minutes" did a story on him.

Good Shepherd Another name for Christ, who really got Satan's goat.

Gospel A term that means "good news"—even though the homily always follows.

grace The prayer you say with your mouth full.

Great Schism A time when there were more Popes than heavyweight boxing champions.

guardian angel   A cherub's cherub.

guilt   Agonizing paranoia some-where along the lines of "God'll get me for what I did." It racks the brain, twists the emotions, and turns the stomach until the person's a physical wreck—and God's job is already done.

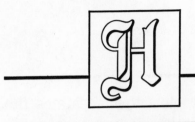

habits Nunderwear.

hagiography Heaven's press guide.

Hail Mary 1. A prayer you say when the answer to the Our Father is "No." 2. The answer to the question, "What would be worse than raining cats and dogs?"

halo The glow that separates the saints from the ain'ts.

Handshake of Peace Shaking hands with the kid next to you in Mass—who just wiped his nose without a handkerchief.

happiness 1. What you feel when a Holy Day of Obligation falls on a Sunday. 2. B-7, I-23, free space, G-58, O-72.

healing, miracle of When a stomachache suddenly goes away because the young patient remembers it's Saturday.

Heaven A place that, according to the song, has no beer—so at least we can count out Milwaukee.

Heaven's Gate A passage that everyone wants to get through and a movie that everyone avoided.

Hell 1. A place even F. Lee Bailey can't save you from. 2. Satan's home on the range.

heresy Bible libel.

heretic 1. Anyone who disagrees with you about something neither one knows anything about. 2. A person who doesn't cry during "It's a Wonderful Life."

High Mass The liturgy attended mainly by those too hung over to make it to an early Mass.

holy cards Pictures of religious figures—like baseball cards without bubble gum.

Holy Day of Obligation 1. As in Monday Night Football, a Mass that counts in the standings. 2. A feast day on which Roman Catholics are duty-bound to suffer through their second Mass, sermon, and collection of the week.

Holy Grail The chalice that Jesus and the Apostles shared at the Last Supper. Its location is unknown and, considering oral hygiene, that's probably for the best.

holy oil Chrism rubbed on the foreheads of teenaged Confirmation candidates—as if they needed any more grease up there.

Holy Saturday The day your knees are sore from Good Friday.

Holy Spirit 1. God making a specter of Himself. 2. The spelling game you play to make Mass pass faster. 3. God: third person singular.

holy water A liquid whose chemical formula is: H_2OLY.

homily The part of Mass when the pastor prepares the flock for the fleecing.

hope A desire that's dashed when Father Talkalot proceeds down the aisle on a hot Sunday.

Host A heavenly treat that's neat to eat.

humility The one virtue you lose the moment that you take credit for it.

hymn A song of praise usually sung in a key three octaves higher than the congregation's range.

hymn, recessional The last song of Mass, often sung a little more quietly since most people have left by that time.

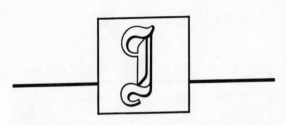

Immaculate Conception 1. A clean thought. 2. The feast that reminds Catholics of the purity of Mary and the fact that they have only seventeen more shopping days until Christmas.

imprimatur What the bishop would never give a book like this.

incense Holy smoke.

indulgence An exemption from sin awarded for a good act, a good deed, or a good chunk of cash.

Innocent III The man who was Pope until Proven Guilty IV.

Inquisition   A tough, *final* exam.

inspiration   How God became the Holy Ghostwriter of the Bible.

intercession   A prayer on behalf of another—although it shouldn't be for the other person to die of hemorrhoids.

Isaac The biblical figure who became anxious when his father, Abraham, wanted to spend some "quality time" with him.

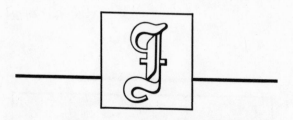

Jesse Tree A plant with religious connections—as opposed to its political relative, the George Bush.

Jesuits An order of priests known for their ability to found colleges with good basketball teams.

Jesus Christ 1. The Son of God who became the Messiah, despite a few cries of nepotism. 2. One person who could truthfully answer yes to the question "Hey, were you born in a barn, or what?"

Jesus freaks The subtitle of the Gospel chapter in which Christ clears the temple.

Jews Known as "The Chosen People." Throughout history, whenever anyone felt the need to pick on someone, they always chose the Jews—if there were no Catholics or gypsies around.

Job A man who probably would have enjoyed root-canal surgery.

John the Baptist 1. The man who started the wet look. 2. The guy your mother told you to stay away from—along with Jim the Lutheran and Chip the Episcopalian.

John the Evangelist The Apostle whose Gospel should be called, "Jesus, Me, and Eleven Other Guys."

Jonah The original "Jaws" story.

Joseph of Arimathea An undertaker who doubled his money by selling Christ a tomb for only three days.

Judas Iscariot 1. The Apostle who didn't realize that it was *his* last supper as well. 2. Someone who left the table without being properly excused.

Judgment Day The day the earth stands still—but everyone else is moving like flies in a microwave.

justice When your kids have kids of their own.

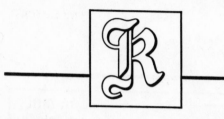

Kingdom of God What always was and always will be—like a holiday fruitcake.

King of the Jews A biblical title that carried about as much weight as being called the most powerful black man in South Africa today.

kiss of death Being Dirty Harry's partner.

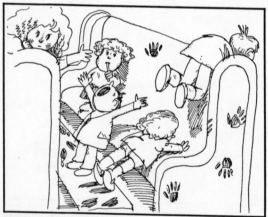

kneeler What little children with muddy shoes love to stand on.

Knights of Columbus The organization responsible for the senseless proliferation of spaghetti dinners.

Kyrie Eleison The only Greek words that most Catholics can recognize besides gyros and baklava.

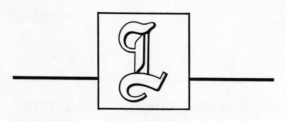

laity Catholics who have Sundays off.

Lamb of God A prayer Catholics can say without missing a bleat.

lapsed Catholic 1. A Catholic who only knows pig Latin. 2. A Catholic who doesn't care if Southern Methodist beats Notre Dame in football.

WHO'S RESPONSIBLE FOR THESE SEATING ARRANGEMENTS?

Last Supper One of the strangest meals in history, because Jesus performed the first Mass and all thirteen in attendance sat on one side of the table.

Latin   The language that died of irregular vowel movements.

Latin Mass   Vatican II—Latin 0.

laying on of hands   A healing action by a charismatic—first on the head, then on the wallet.

lay ministry Nonclergy who help out with affairs of the Church.

Lazarus 1. A friend of Jesus' who died but got better. 2. A man who was late for his own funeral.

WOULD YOU MIND TAKING OFF YOUR SPORT COAT? I CAN'T HEAR THE LECTOR!

lector The liturgical reader who must be able to speak louder than the sport coats of the ushers.

Lent 1. The time of year when you borrow ham sandwiches from your Protestant neighbors. 2. The last chance before summer to keep those broken New Year's promises.

"Let my people go!" The line that catapulted the Israelites into freedom and Charlton Heston into stardom.

lie A misrepresentation that should be confessed in church and improved on the golf course.

life after death When human beings go into syndication.

limbo A place for unbaptized souls who must bend over backwards to get into Heaven.

Litany The part of the Mass you don't need to memorize.

liturgy Just about the only urgy that can be satisfied by an unmarried Catholic.

Lord's Prayer God's only endorsed product.

Lot How much salt there is in a pillar.

"Love thy neighbor as thyself" The Golden Rule—for everyone except masochists.

lust One of the seven deadly sins— confessed to a man who is not allowed to commit it.

lyre   A biblical instrument that masqueraded as a harp.

Madonna Latin for "like a virgin."

Magi The most famous trio ever to attend a baby shower.

mammon Material goods, which the Church says you can't serve while serving God. This from a multibillion-dollar institution that doesn't pay taxes.

manger 1. Where Mary gave birth to Jesus because Joseph wasn't covered by an HMO. 2. The Bible's way of showing us that holiday travel has always been rough.

manna The trail of bread crumbs that God left for the Israelites until they could find their way out of the desert.

martyr 1. Someone dying to be a saint. 2. A religious person who gets stoned.

Mary, Blessed Virgin The only mother who ever became well-known for her virginity.

Mary Magdalene The woman the disciples greeted with "How's tricks?"

Mass The kind of confusion that exists in the church parking lot every Sunday.

Mass attendance How young adult Catholics "pay the rent" when they still live with their parents.

masturbation   Fiddling while Rome burns.

materialism   A sin that American Catholics are preoccupied with—according to the guy with his own city.

mea culpa   An obscure way to take the blame for something without letting everyone know that you screwed up.

"The meek shall inherit the earth" The Lord's trickle-down theory.

mercy   When there is no sermon on a hot Sunday.

Messiah A classical piece that Catholics have a Handel on.

Methodists Protestants who go by the Book.

Methuselah The oldest man in history at 969 years old, which is 6,783 in dog years.

Middle Ages When a Catholic is old enough to go to Mass alone, but still has to bring home a bulletin as proof.

Minister of Hospitality How the usher describes his job to the maintenance engineer.

minor prophets The kind of seers you can find at Sears.

miracle 1. A Catholic family with fewer than six kids. 2. An event with no reasonable explanation—such as "The Honeymooners: The Lost Episodes." 3. Divine intervention—prayed for most ardently in the waning seconds of football games.

missal A book of hymns and haws.

missalettes The dancing girls at progressive masses.

missions   1. The Church's branch offices. 2. Religious organizations that go to underdeveloped countries and give the natives one more thing to be restless about.

mitre   The hat that the bishop has to take off at the movies.

monks   What priests evolved from.

monotheism　When God speaks to you over the AM dial of your radio.

monsignor　A title conferred by the Pope on a priest that grants him an extra ten minutes of sermon per week.

mortal sin　A sin which your parents would kill you for, if they found out.

mortification　Ignoring your stomach growls during Mass.

Mosaic Law Rules that shouldn't be hard to enforce considering the ten plagues.

Moses The leader of the Israelites who should have gone up the mountain a third time for directions out of the desert.

Mount of Olives A hill located near the Strait of Vermouth.

Mount Sinai The place where God told Moses to take two tablets and call Him in the morning.

movable feast The parish meals-on-wheels program.

myrrh The second gift of the Magi, and a great Scrabble™ word when you're out of vowels.

Mysteries of the Church Phenomena that are impossible to understand. For example, how a five-foot-tall altar boy can lift a twenty-pound book high enough for an eighty-year-old man to read from.

Mysteries of the Rosary Things to ponder while you're praying the rosary—such as how to get the darned thing untangled.

Nazareth   Jesus' mailing address.

New Testament   Sequel to the Old Testament in which God was in a considerably better mood.

Noah   A story about a man and his dogs—and his elephants, his giraffes, his armadillos ....

Noah's Ark   A combination of "Wild Kingdom" and "The Love Boat."

novices   Clerics who are still adjusting their habits.

Numbers, Book of   What Moses called his little black book.

nun 1. A woman who has taken vows of poverty and chastity—hence the name. 2. The butt of the joke ending with this punch line: "That was no laity, that was my sister."

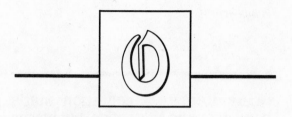

obedience The vow of "monk he see, monk he do."

offering A sacrifice unto God— hangovers not included.

Old Testament A book of scripts for Cecil B. De Mille.

olive branch A welcome sign of hope for Noah, since he had only stocked enough martini olives for thirty-eight days.

omnipotence   A condition that's better than the alternative, but just as hard to treat.

omnipresence   The principle that explains why your parents always walk into the TV room during the dirtiest part of the movie.

omniscience   God's ability to know everything—and the reason that whatever goes in the collection plate, stays in the collection plate.

One (1) A.D.   The year people's ages finally started increasing each year.

ordinary time   The period on the liturgical calendar when the Church readily admits that there isn't much going on.

Original Sin   1. What is cleansed by baptism, after which we use the new and improved kind. 2. What teenagers are always trying to come up with.

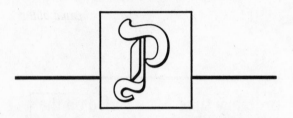

pagans People without religion whose numbers span the globe— never knowing the thrill of a bingo victory or the agony of the feet after the reading of the Passion.

palms Branches you leave behind in the pews on Palm Sunday, only to have the priest burn them and rub the cinders on your forehead the next Ash Wednesday.

Palm Sunday The Sunday before Easter, also called Passion Sunday— but don't hold your breath.

pantheism The belief in the miracle of Teflon™.

papal audience An event so popular that you can only get tickets from scalpers.

papal brief What the Pope wears under his vestments when he runs out of clean papal boxers.

papal bull A letter from the Pope that's infallibull.

papal infallibility   1. The doctrine which states that the only time the Pope is wrong is when he thinks he's mistaken. 2. Why the Pope would clean up on "Jeopardy."

papal legate   A representative of the Pontiff with limited authority—in other words, a Pope-on-a-rope.

papal visit   When countries roll out the red carpet and half their GNP for the Pope—who tells them to do something about the poor.

parable   The format used to make a short story long.

paradise A place so perfect that you are either dreaming or dead.

parish The church where you are so well known that you can't go there for confession.

parochial school Where you learn enough about religion to say Mass and enough about sex to use the right public restroom.

Passion of Christ The rags-to-riches-to-rags story of a drifter who rode into town and stayed too long.

paten The communion plate which the altar boy uses to core your Adam's apple.

patience A virtue that Catholics forget to practice once they reach the church parking lot.

patron saint The guardian you talk to when all of God's lines are busy.

penance What you need to get to the Afterworld Series.

Pentateuch The first five books of the Bible—and the only books of the Old Testament that Catholics can recall.

Pentecost Fifty days after Easter—by which time you've more than made up for your Lenten sacrifices.

permanent deacon A married man who can do almost anything a priest can, and some things he can't.

petitions The time during Mass when everyone is praying for world peace but thinking "Please help me win the lottery."

pew 1. A medieval torture device still found in Catholic churches. 2. A real pain in the Mass.

Pharisees A Jewish sect that was always trying to trap Jesus with questions—like a biblical Phil Donahue or William F. Buckley, Jr.

piety A quality respected in a clergyman but suspected in anyone else.

pilgrim A traveler who couldn't afford a real vacation.

pious A Cathoholic.

plenary indulgence A get-out-of-purgatory-free card.

Pontius Pilate   A grown man whose wife still had to tell him when to wash his hands.

Pope   Bishop of Rome and Vicar of Jesus Christ, Successor of St. Peter, Prince of the Apostles, Supreme Pontiff of the Universal Church, Patriarch of the West, Primate of Italy, Archbishop and Metropolitan of the Roman Province, Sovereign of Vatican City, and all-around Great Goy.

possession 1. A condition that requires plenty of fresh air and exorcise. 2. A condition that turns heads.

poverty A vow taken by the clergy that keeps the Church in the black.

prayer Your last resort for obtaining something that you don't have a chance in Hell of getting.

preaching When someone **else** is telling **you** what's moral.

Pre-Cana The required wedding preparation retreat which helps a couple establish a solid base for arguments in the coming years of marriage.

predestination 1. The rendezvous spot for you and your friends when you're supposed to be at Mass. 2.The gas station where a Catholic family stops, even though Mom and Dad told everyone to go before they left.

Presbyterians Protestants who can spell.

pride Bringing photographs along to confession.

priest A spiritual adviser, conductor of church services, and a good reference on a college application.

procession The ceremonial formation at the beginning of Mass, consisting of the altar boys, the lay ministers, the celebrant, and the late parishioners looking for a seat.

Prodigal Son A parable with a happy ending for everyone but the fatted calf.

prophet A man who, 3,000 years ago, predicted events that took place 2,000 years ago—and whom we're supposed to believe today.

Protestant A person who will probably make it to Heaven, but won't live in as good a neighborhood.

prudence The virtue you are not practicing when you try to borrow money from the collection plate.

purgatory 1. A place that Cub fans will bypass completely. 2. A place where a snowball still has a chance.

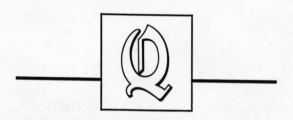

"Quo Vadis?" Latin for "whither dost thou go?" The answer: on to the next letter, as this is the only *Q* term.

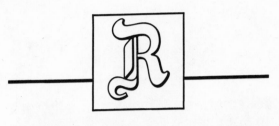

rationalize The way most Catholics prefer to cleanse themselves of sin.

recessional The ceremonial procession at the conclusion of Mass—led by parishioners trying to beat the crowd to the parking lot.

rectory secretary The lady the pastor calls in to take the benediction.

redemption When you finally cash in your chips.

Reformation When Catholic kids have to make space in their rooms for a new brother or sister.

relics People who have been going to Mass for so long they actually know when to sit, kneel, and stand.

religion A cult with a good PR department.

religious calling 1. A yell on the bell to keep people out of Hell. 2. When Jehovah's Witnesses come a-knockin'.

religious superior A person created a little more equal than you.

Renunciation of the Devil Turning out the light on the Prince of Darkness.

Resurrection of Christ It's hard to keep a good Man down.

retribution When whatsoever you do to the least of your brothers is done back to you.

revelation When children are told that there is no Santa Claus, no Easter Bunny, and that they have to attend Mass every Sunday for the rest of their lives.

Revelation The final book of the Bible, which doesn't exactly end "and they lived happily ever after."

rhythm method Why Catholic kids don't have rooms of their own.

Rome Where II and II is IV.

rosary A prayer ritual that seems to last five decades.

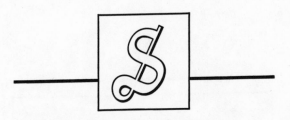

Sabbath A day of worship and rest, meaning Mass and football (in no particular order).

sacrament An after-sinner mint.

Sacrament of Baptism The first time the Church soaks you.

Sacrament of Confirmation The sacrament for which you need a sponsor—although the Church frowns on STP™ or Pennzoil™.

Sacrament of Holy Eucharist The liturgical breadline.

Sacrament of Holy Orders When God wants **you.**

Sacrament of Matrimony 1. The sacrament that entitles a man and a woman to live together—which some priests refuse to administer to couples who are already living together. 2. The chief cause of unholy divorce.

Sacrament of Reconciliation Solemnly asking forgiveness for actions you wish you had videotaped to show your friends.

Sacrament of the Sick The sacrament for which no one bothers to buy you a gift.

sacrifice What a father makes when his child's First Communion interferes with his tee time.

sacrilege Irreverent use of something sacred—but it's too late now, you're already up to the *S*'s.

sacristy 1. The clerical locker room. 2. A place where divestment is not a moral issue.

saint A person always pictured as light-headed.

Saint Anthony The saint a man prays to when his wife can't find what he's looking for.

Saint Basil A man for all seasonings.

Saint Catherine Choose one.

Saint Christopher The saint to call if AAA doesn't answer.

Saint Joan of Arc The patron saint of Camp Fire Girls.

Saint Joseph 1. The husband of the Virgin Mary and patron saint of cold showers. 2. The most boring role in the Christmas pageant.

Saint Jude   The patron saint of the federal budget.

Saint Paul   The patron saint of a large midwestern city.

Saint Peter   The Apostle that Jesus once called "The Rock"—now employed as the bouncer at the Pearly Gates.

Satan   An angel who got fired.

savior   A person willing to die for others—hence the shortage.

scapular   A distinctive part of the priest's uniform that enables us to tell which team he's praying for.

scribes   The men who covered the Christ story for the tabloids.

scripture Writings that Christ used as an appointment book.

Second Coming When you had better not be standing anywhere near the fan.

seminary The place where novices practice what they'll preach.

sermon 1. The part of the Mass that begins with a recap of the Gospel and then drones into other gray matters of Christianity while your gray matter wanders off into subjects such as whether there are still the same number of ceiling tiles as last week. 2. Another word for homily, which doesn't make it any shorter.

Sermon on the Mount Where Christ delivered a speech, provided food for the hungry multitude, and actually collected the remainder so that nothing went to waste—a good lesson for all politicians.

sexual intercourse A caring, special act between two people who are in love, married (to each other), in bed, under the covers, with the lights off, and the door locked—for the purpose of creating more Catholics.

A SHEKEL FOR YOUR THOUGHTS.

RODIN'S THE THINKER

shekel The going rate for a thought in biblical times.

shroud Pajamas for the big sleep.

Shroud of Turin An old burial garment that Christ wouldn't be caught dead in.

Sign of the Cross 1. How young Catholics remember which hand is their right one. 2. A gesture showing reverence for the Cross—used during Mass and before free-throws.

Simon of Cyrene The guy who ran the second leg in the crucifixion relay.

sin A reprehensible act that can be categorized as either venial (e.g., maliciously breaking a window) or mortal (e.g., maliciously breaking a stained-glass church window).

sinner Someone who cannot cast the first stone, but would be more than happy to hurl the next five or six.

sin of commission An action that is immoral, such as picking all the cashews out of the holiday nut mix.

sin of omission ...never putting any cashews in the nut mix in the first place.

Sistine Chapel Proof that you should never hire a guy with only one name to paint your ceiling.

sloth The cardinal sin of laziness—which can only be forgiven by a guy who works one day a week.

sodality A religious organization that you join to dress up your application to Heaven.

Sodom and Gomorrah Where Old Testament college students went on spring break.

Solomon A man known for his wisdom, despite the fact that he had three hundred wives.

Son of God Why Jesus would clean up in all the events at biblical Father and Son picnics.

Son of Man A term that must have added to the confusion Jesus felt on Father's Day.

state of grace After you receive absolution, but before you see a cute girl genuflecting.

Sunday 1. The day you get burned if you are not in Church. 2. The day you sleep in and go to Mass—trying not to do them simultaneously.

synagogue Where Jesus is just another pretty face.

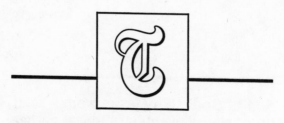

tabernacle   Where Christ had an out-of-body experience.

temperance   1. The virtue of moderation, which many Catholics practice in their Mass attendance. 2. The attitude that no booze is good booze.

temptation   A condition conducive to sinning—for most people, just being conscious.

Temptation of Christ To once, just once, declare "To hell with what the Scriptures say, Peter, *I* say we're going to the beach today."

Ten Commandments The most important Top Ten list not given by Casey Kasem.

theologian 1. A sage who writes at length about how little we know of God. 2. Someone who would know where Noah kept the termites.

theology The college course that helps you unlearn all the things you learned in religion class.

tithing Donating 10% of your income to the Church or losing even more at weekly bingo games.

Tower of Babel The reason why the Lord created different languages. He scattered the builders across the continent, only to have them reunite in New York as cabbies.

transcendence, divine A gift given to Jesus—and Shirley MacLaine, too.

Transfiguration of Christ When Scotty used the wrong coordinates and almost beamed up Jesus.

Trappists A monastic order that catches its own food—except during Lent, because it's pretty tough to snare a grilled-cheese sandwich.

Trinity 1. The doctrine that God is three persons in one, which gives Catholic students a handicap in Logic 101. 2. Three Gods, no waiting.

trust in God Words the Church firmly believes in (especially on legal tender).

"turn the other cheek" The rule of thumb when the other guy is bigger.

Unitarians Protestants who believe in individual freedom of belief. They're considering changing their name to Diversarians.

Urban II A Pope who lived inside the Vatican City limits, in contrast to a later Pope, Suburban I, the Commuter Pope.

ushers The only people in the parish who don't know the seating capacity of a pew.

Vacation Bible School How parents ruin a child's summer vacation.

Valley of the Shadow of Death The trendy part of Hell where girls say things like "omySatan" and "gag me with a pitchfork."

Vatican City The only country which will never win an Olympic luge medal.

vespers Vat ve hear ven vorshippers don't vant to vear out their velcome.

vestments Sunday clothes—for priests, a cassock and surplice; for ushers, a polyester leisure suit.

vigil Looking out for Number One.

vine and branches   A biblical metaphor: Christ is the vine, we are the branches—and the Big Guy has the pruners.

virgin birth   Paying the fiddler without getting to dance.

virginity   What cannot be refunded once a deposit is made.

virtues   Qualities that help people do what is morally right—although the Church does not officially include "fear" on the list.

visions   What you see after too much sacramental wine.

vocation   A job with an eternal retirement plan.

vow The only way a Catholic can swear.

Vulgate The version of the Bible that Spock reads.

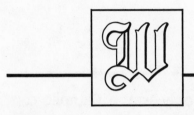

walking on water What was considered a miracle for Jesus on the Sea of Galilee, but is no trick at all on Lake Erie.

walls of Jericho Where Joshua brought the house down with his music.

"The Way, the Truth, and the Light" Three obstacles that you must surmount when sneaking into the house at night.

Wedding at Cana Where Christ warmed up before He took His show on the road.

wine 1. What you see on the altar and hear in the cry room. 2. The grapes of Mass.

Wojtyla, Karol The reason Pope John Paul II changed his name.

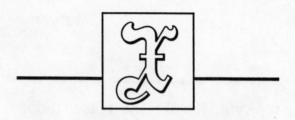

Xavier, Saint A missionary saint who is always mentioned in dictionaries because he supplies the only *X* word.

Yahweh Like Abba and Jehovah, another name for God who uses so many names you'd think he was wanted somewhere for something.

Yom Kippur 1. The only day of the year when Catholics can eat anything and Jews can eat nothing. 2. Who Jewish university football teams win one for.

TROCAIRE COLLEGE
Buffalo, New York 14220

Zacchaeus A tax man who claimed the first business lunch write-off.

Zion According to the song, what the harvest moon should do.

OTHER MURPHY'S
AW

by Bruce Lansky

The wit of Bombeck and the wisdom of Murphy are combined in this collection of 325 laws that detail the perils and pitfalls of parenthood. Cartoon illustrations by Christine Tripp.
$.50
Ordering #: 1149

MOTHER MURPHY'S
2nd LAW

by Bruce Lansky
A ribald collection of laws about love, sex, marriage and other skirmishes that can't be found in marriage or sex manuals.
$2.95
Ordering #: 4010

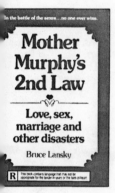

OW TO SURVIVE HIGH
CHOOL WITH MINIMAL
RAIN DAMAGE

by Doug Lansky and
Aaron Dorfman

The hilarious guide for high school students that tells how to be cool in high school. It contains hundreds of pranks, hoaxes and dirty tricks. It's "the greatest invention for high school kids since Cliffs Notes."
Dave Barry. $4.95
Ordering #: 4050

GRANDMA KNOWS BEST BUT NO ONE EVER LISTENS
by Mary McBride
Mary McBride instructs grandmas who have been stuc with babysitting how to "schem lie, cheat, and threaten so you'll be thought of as a sweet, darling grandma." **$4.95**
Ordering #: 4009

DON'T CALL MOMMY TODAY UNLESS THE SITTER RUNS AWAY
by Mary McBride with Veronica McBride
The McBrides give hilarious advice to mothers who leave their children in daycare, in school or in front of the TV as they pursue the glory of a career. "More valuable to the working mother than a cart full of frozen dinners."—Phyllis Diller. **$4.95**
Ordering #: 4039

THE EMPTY NEST SYMPHONY
by Mary McBride with Veronica McBride
This humorous guide to life aft the kids have moved out takes all the pains out of birthdays that occur after the thirty-nint and will add a few laugh lines t even the most serious faces. **$4.95**
Ordering #: 4080

WALL STREET BULL

by Bruce Lansky

The latest expose to rock Wall Street is a humorous lexicon of over 500 words commonly heard in Wall Street boardrooms and barrooms...and what they really mean. It exposes the gallows humor that lies at the heart of Wall Street bull. **$4.95**

Ordering #: 4040

LEXICON OF INTENTIONALLY AMBIGUOUS RECOMMENDATIONS (L.I.A.R.)

by Robert Thornton

This witty guide can help you give a good recommendation to someone who can't manage his own sock drawer—and still tell the truth. Anyone who has ever had to write a recommendation needs this book. "Scathing condemnations that can be read as ringing praise."—Harry Reasoner, CBS News Broadcast. **$4.95**

Ordering #: 4070

ITALIAN WITHOUT WORDS

by Don Cangelosi and Joseph Delli Carpini

An ingenious invention that's a must for every Italian, traveler to Italy or visitor to Little Italys throughout America. This humorous "phrase book" without words contains the most common gestures and body language that enables anyone to communicate nonverbally in Italian. **$3.95**

Ordering #: 5100

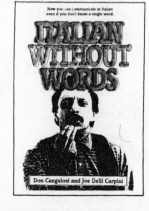

ORDER FORM

Qty.	Order #	Book Title	Author	Price
____	5090	Asian Customs and Manners	Chambers	$7.95
____	5070	Best European Travel Tips	Whitman	$6.95
____	1049	David, We're Pregnant	Johnston	$4.95
____	4039	Don't Call Mommy at Work	McBride	$4.95
____	1089	Do They Ever Grow Up?	Johnston	$4.95
____	4080	Empty Nest Symphony	McBride	$4.95
____	5080	European Customs and Manners	Braganti/Devine	$6.95
____	2190	Free Stuff for Kids	FS Editors	$3.95
____	4009	Grandma Knows Best	McBride	$4.95
____	1139	Hi Mom! Hi Dad!	Johnston	$4.95
____	4020	How to Find Romance in the Personals	Price/Dana	$4.95
____	4050	How to Survive High School	Lansky/Dorfman	$4.95
____	5100	Italian Without Words	Cangelosi/ Carpini	$3.95
____	1289	Letters From a Pregnant Coward	Armor	$6.95
____	4070	L.I.A.R.	Thornton	$4.95
____	1149	Mother Murphy's Law	Lansky	$3.50
____	4010	Mother Murphy's 2nd Law	Lansky	$2.95
____	4060	Papal Bull	Sullivan	$4.95
____	4040	Wall Street Bull	Lansky	$4.95
____	6030	Webster's Dictionary Game	Webster	$5.95

Please send me copies of the books checked above. I am enclosing $_____ which covers the full amount per book shown above plus $1.25 for postage and handling for the first book and $.50 for each additional book. (Add $2.00 to total for books shipped to Canada. Overseas postage and handling will be billed. MN residents add 6% sales tax.) Allow up to four weeks for delivery. Send check or money order payable to Meadowbrook, Inc. No cash or C.O.D.'s please. **Quantity discounts available upon request.**

For purchases over $10.00, you may use VISA or MasterCard

☐ MasterCard   Account #_____Exp. Date_____

☐ VISA   Signature_____

Name_____

Address_____

City_____State_____Zip_____
s/a:03

Meadowbrook, Inc., 18318 Minnetonka Boulevard, Deephaven, MN 55391, (612) 473-5400, Toll free (800) 338-2232.